FAMOUS ROADKILL

FAMOUS ROADKILL

Allan Safarik

HAGIOS PRESS

Library and Archives Canada Cataloguing in Publication

Safarik, Allan, 1948-
    Famous Roadkill / Allan Safarik.

Poems.
ISBN 978-1-926710-16-7

I. Title.

PS8587.A245F34 2012   C811'.54   C2012-901531-8

Edited by Paul Wilson.
Designed and typeset by Donald Ward.
Cover art: "Po's Sorrow," by Marsha Kennedy.
Cover design by Tanya Wolk, Go Giraffe Go Inc.
Set in Minion Pro.
Printed and bound in Canada.

The publishers gratefully acknowledge the assistance of the Saskatchewan Arts Board, The Canada Council for the Arts, and the Cultural Industries Development Fund (Saskatchewan Department of Culture, Youth & Recreation) in the production of this book.

HAGIOS PRESS
Box 33024 Cathedral PO
Regina SK   S4T 7X2
www.hagiospress.com

In memory of Gary Hyland

ACKNOWLEDGEMENTS

These poems were written in 2011 in the historic Jacoby
House (1906) in Dundurn, Saskatchewan. A quiet location in
a rural town 35 km south of Saskatoon just off the Number
11 Highway. "Markers Beside the Road" was first published
in The Society. "Neon at the Outskirts at the Break of Dawn"
first appeared in Everyday Poems. This volume is dedicated
to the memory of Gary Hyland, the Poets' Poet, literary pro-
moter and community builder par excellence. With thanks to
the Regina artist Marsha Kennedy for the use of her picture
on the cover. Once again Dolores Reimer was enlisted to
protect me from falling off the edge. Books are a collaborative
effort and I wish to thank Paul Wilson for his editing skills
and Don Ward for his mastery of typesetting and design. I
would also like to thank The Saskatchewan Arts Board for
a grant that allowed me the time to work full-time on this
manuscript for a number of months.

CONTENTS

I. DRYLAND

II. FURTHER NOTES

I. DRYLAND

INVOCATION TO THE FRONT DOOR

Here I am living in isolation in the middle
of the biggest wheat field in the universe
Yet, I expect someone daily to knock on the door
come in and sit a while over coffee and cake
and tell me what the people in town are saying
about lousy weather or the muddy roads.
Sometimes I peer out the keyhole to see
if anybody unexpected is about to arrive
or impulsively I walk over to the threshold
and jar the door open suddenly to surprise
whoever isn't about to enter the room.

When somebody really does show up
I peer out around the curtains as if to say
"Who are you and what do you want?"
while the dog runs up and down in front
of the window barking and barking as if
nobody could possibly be at home.
I'm in the living room in my underwear
reading a book and a poem is starting
to work on my brain like a hand grabbing
a fistful of dough and beating it flat
on a laminated board sprinkled with flour.

On occasion, I open you with great ceremony
because I am honoured by the thought
someone wants to cross your threshold
just to come inside to visit with me.
I keep them waiting for a decent interval
while the dog goes wild in his excitement.
Then yawning sheepishly I appear disoriented
looking as if I just got up from my nap
and you open with groaning reverence

and the person waiting there is so startled
at my sudden dishevelled appearance
that they start to back away as if to apologise
but the big silver kettle in the kitchen's already
singing brightly hello, hello my friend welcome.

GERMINATION

It continues snowing in May
the miserable rooster
crows at the crack of noon
the Hutterite egg man
collects the twenty bucks
still owed from the last box
of extra large eggs

His ninety year old
mother-in-law died in the night
Later, I see her image staring
up at me from the kitchen sink
pale in the coarse shroud
white alfalfa sprouts
growing on her chin

DREAM OF BUTTERMILK

Clouds the colour of sheep cheese
a lone thistle wears an old man's beard
many grey flies walk backwards in the dust
The rusty water pump imitates the noise
oars in oarlocks make rowing down
the middle of the wind torn lake
Weather leaking in my shirt pocket
turns the water fountain-pen-blue

A stain as difficult as blood scrubbed
from a cotton shirt with a copper brush
after a soaking in vinegar and iodine
In the field during goose hunting season
a farmer shot an angel over his decoys
set out on swathes staring into the wind
He plucked the down into a paper bag
one pellet hole in the buttermilk breast

THE MAWSON TRAIL

Deer cross the back road just out from the edge of town
a hundred times a day coming and going between the bush
and flooded grain fields that line the underside of the sky
Many geese in formal grey suits wander around gabbling
like crazy Irish priests in search of a flock of devout believers
question mark necks punctuate the squawking litany
before the loquacious ones lift off on beating flight pinions

Coyote sitting on the bush line watches the proceedings
like an ubiquitous host who wishes to dine out
with friends but has none, only an urge that tells him
to never pine away because trial, error and repetition
mean dinner's sometimes served in unexpected places
a ham sandwich tossed from a school bus window
or a suicidal bunny caught in a loop of invisible wire

Just when a hungry brain thinks it's down and out
in the midst of plenty, it's forced to go down by the water
to try and catch a small brown frog gingerly crunched
with front teeth before snapping it down with real panache
rewarded by another feast in a piping plover nest
looking more like a handful of speckled granite
than a clutch of eggs playing at simple camouflage

Many small meals until he can get back on his usual diet
of roadkill dying every few days under rubber wheels
a tax for living high on the back of the proverbial hog
The sound of machinery drives him off fresh meat
while crows who also pray for convenient death
hopping up and down in a mercurial dance routine
take off and hover in the wind like black flags

BIG DEAD MYSTERY

gas leaking slowly from the gut bag
stinks up the whole neighbourhood
who thought you could shoot something
this large and leave it out in the street?

nobody owed up to the awful truth
it's just that some people believe
there should be laws about the size
of the pets people keep in their yards

after all there are noise bylaws and rules
about the height of fences and roof lines
and on which days lawns can be watered
and regulations about rental suites

the bylaw officer went door to door
making discrete inquiries about gun shots
and which way the wind was blowing
turned out to be a blue bird afternoon

nobody heard or saw anything suspicious
only a pair of ravens playing in the street
a red road hockey net and a tennis ball
left from the game the night before

folks figured they followed it into town
from one of the farms on the back road
where the shooter gut shot it fervently
hoping it would go elsewhere to die

AN HOUR AFTER DARK

As many frogs
as stars sing in the
meadow under water

Heat quickly leaves
an ancient boulder
cooling in the shade

No glorification
of the landscape
without the sun

UNDER THE COVER OF THE WINDY NIGHT

Dark trees stream and jostle against the force
Land all around beaten down by flattening wind
Punished long grass doubled over by the weight
Of invisible blows and the dusty spit of cold rain
Turning immense rivers of sand into clinging mud

In the woodshed the black widow weaves a web
A pack rat looks for a way into the ramshackle house
Pigeons, furtive lovers coo under the roof's overhang
An agitated dog barks at the warp in the window glass
Smoke is yanked like a scared rabbit from the chimney

No reason for light to ever enter the world again
Sound batters the half asleep brain until it wakes
Chaos reins in logic, luckily dreams are illogical
Thunder rolls across the parched brown fields
Deep voice of stone revered from ancient times

THE VEGETABLE MAN

The onion man went out
to dig up an onion and fell
into the neighbour's grave
that had accidentally blown open
and drifted down to the wrong
end of the field somehow
crossing a fence line passing
through a small stand of trees
before it stopped in his veggies

It took him all day to get out
from inside the six foot hole
aided by a wandering dog
he befriended that pulled him
out yanking on his shirt collar
while he stood on his tippy toes
on the top of the mahogany box

When he got home he had a nap
because he was tired from jumping
up and down trying to become
tall enough to give his new pal
something substantial to grab onto
in the morning when he finally
woke up and went out to look
the grave had gone back home

There was no reason for it
nothing happened here
that had not happened
hundreds maybe thousands
of times in the history
of the unbelievable world
one raw freshly pulled onion
changes just about every
possible relationship that exists
in an unsure world where
death's only an onion away

BALD TREES

The yellow trees
ready to drop
their leaves.

One good blow
they'll turn
into hard,
bald suckers
like small town
truck drivers or
the military
police.

Fall, a few weeks
waiting
for winter.

Most wives move out
this time of year
leaving the old
bald bastard flat
by the time
the leaves
drop dead.

Can you blame them?
Who'd want to listen
to that, breathing
in the dark?

WILD TURKEY

Mix-up in the bar
nothing much
to report

a dead man
came in looking
for an old
drinking buddy

found him
in the arms
of his widow

a week later
it happened again
when wind blew
in the back door

the woman
who smells of
cinnamon sticks
puking
in the corner

the same black
dog had her
by the sleeve

DOG'S HEAD BARKING

What do you want to do
with the legs and the tail?
Dunno know but I'll put
the snarling head in my
front window to surprise
the town man when he
comes to read the meter

He'll look in and flip out
at the nasty teeth
the red gash where
the neck left off
Word will get out
at coffee row I'm nuts
They'll stop giving me
the Don Cherry salute
when I drive by

That's life in the country
a severed dog's head
in a porch window
Soon news spreads
about an unusual pet
no hind legs, not much
in the way of front end

That's okay there's
nothing to feed or walk
it will never run off
or bother the neighbour's
garbage or chase cats
One thing sure, never
have to buy a collar

22   *Allan Safarik*

JACKFISH CUISINE

Big hook in the jackfish body
holds separating bones
twenty lbs of rainbow bruises
rots on a rope in a tree
skin on the greasy carcass
erupting into fish acne

Foul hooked through slack skin
early morning in the slough
back of the old red cow barn
south of the crossroads

An airforce of angry wasps
hover around the heat source
darting in and around the flesh
under the buttery sun

"When it gets good and rank
we're going to preserve
it in wide mouth mason jars
in thick tomato sauce."

Old Art the dog catcher
told me as he proudly
posed for a photo
with his prized catch

"Imagine all the good
eating when the January
snow has landed on the roof
and it's minus forty in the shade.
I left the guts inside to give it
that just right gamey taste

of a good fish snagged
on a hot August day."

I moved him a little to the left
so I could get the neighbour's
hungry orange cat yowling
on the top of the fence
into the picture's frame

THINKING ABOUT SASKATOON

some people, especially Americans
think the word a hilarious accident
somebody invented to fool
the tongue into speaking foreign

I know what they mean watching
the brittle green trees, the damp
river moving sluggishly by in June
mute geese at rest on a sand bar

COUNTING CHICKENS

Suckers who fell for it lined up
for a special demonstration
in front of the new fangled
solar powered plucking machine
on a truck outside the RM office.
They go to coffee row and
talk about it until they slosh
then all over again at church.

Daughters in the country
locked away for a reason
mostly to do with the sins
of past generations staring
out from frames on stained
wallpaper in tall stairwells.
They are allowed out when
their knuckles have grown
swollen on angry red hands.

Sons, mostly inarticulate
always on time for dinner
until they stop entirely coming
into the house from the steady
familiar layout of the barn
or stay way out in the field
on the speck of a tractor pulling
a harrow through the clods
returning well after darkness
clatters down from the sky.

Back at it before dawn
because he has to repair
the hinges or whatever
parts malfunctioned to lift
the black wall from the field
to get the sun up on time
and the white chickens stirring.
It's a big responsibility
living in the country.

COFFEE ROW

You're not telling me a tall tale are ya?
Wouldn't be the first or last big story
you repeated changing the names
I'm like an old sock on a cold foot
not enough yarn to darn my holes
You know what I'm talking about
dontcha? There's only one place like it
down south at the edge of the country
Some say at the very end of memory
There's always one who knows
the question to the correct answer
Sometimes it happens to snow in July
Not every year but often enough

It's just like a farmer's daughter
to chase the dog in a summer blizzard
until the liver spots drop off his sides
and the flowers pack up their petals
Why it was pure hell on the mosquitoes
they disappeared like little black lies
lost in nature's elocution lessons
when the wind carried them off
The sound of car doors slamming
and the metal jangle of the freight
pulling a river of metal through town
scared up the pigeons on the tracks
circling until they were lost in the sun
Take a good look at my face is anything
drastically out of place?

    Allan Safarik

MARKERS BESIDE THE ROAD

Passing through the country
miles of yellow canola flowers
covered with dancing bees
Stopped to have a closer look
thirsty road side margins frame
the edges of consciousness
Invisible mosquitoes come
swarming from the grass
bound for bloody glory or bust
Slapping with both hands
plaster the dead on my face
stuck like small winged scars
I shuffle back into the car
leaving footprints in the dust

In the ditch a white cross
bearing a wreath of faded plastic
flowers and the letters RIP
An eighteen wheeler hauling
through sways in the breeze
flinging a clatter of pebbles
where the story begins
or unfolds in the journey
Sameness of time stops
here again to pause briefly
at this spot for whatever reason
A ribbon of white birds
wraps up the unfinished sky

BLACK RIVER DOGS

Call it mystery in the summer heat
a mirage makes an image of water
pure white sea birds soar above
a transparent cigarette paper flutters
away from a tortured shaking hand
drops of sweat fall like spitting rain
the traveller takes the thirsty trail
black crickets crawl across the sand
hawk catches a snake in burnt grass

Choices are simple in this country
there's never a shortage of weather
wipe away the dust with your sleeve
no use trying to go back into time
the sun fades everything dead drab
nobody around here tells the truth
either there's water or there's not
in a stick nest in a wind twisted tree
two magpies gamble for your soul

STANDING IN THE LIGHT

It's not your fault the trees
here are so tall they obscure.
Somebody built the stone wall
right around the property
before you were born.

The river jumped its banks
a dozen times in the past
twenty-five or thirty years;
take your choice because
history will make it right.

Correction and judgement
make passing comments
when they are necessary.
The church spire on the hill
visible for ten miles.

WHITE TAILS IN EVERY DIRECTION

Over the hood of the car
behind the rear wheels
elegant jumpers
with hang time above
the wire fence lines
both sides of the road
bounding into the bush
white tails grow on trees

Like the man with the red
handkerchief in his back
pocket everybody in town
glimpsed in a blink of the eye
along back lanes, picking
bottles in highway ditches
leaping out from dumpsters
mopping a sun red brow

FAMOUS ROADKILL

Sun glare afternoon
clock ticking in my head
until a vision briefly stops
the second hand dead
from its relentless march

Hovering on an updraft
over the other lane
a Great Horned Owl
glances off the mirror
on an oncoming truck

Nothing in dispute
wings flap hysterically
on the gravel edge
time falls back into place
clicking into its groove

Wind pushes the car
aside like a rowboat
on a river of asphalt
hood ornament chrome
shine irritates the sky

THE INCIDENT

Old man Wilts was home tucking
into a turkey dinner with all the trimmings
when the police came pounding
on his kitchen door to tell him his cows
were out on the Number 11 Highway.
By Golly he had just poured the gravy
onto his Yukon Gold mashed potatoes.
When he got out there he saw a cow
on its side in the ditch and a banged up SUV
that had run through the barbed wire fence.

The cows were kicking up their heels
in a chorus line in the right hand lane
trucks were gliding by like wind ships
covered with coloured running lights.
He got panicky when the cop started
yelling so he went to his truck pulled out
his 30/30 and shot all five cows dead.
The cop hit the ditch calling for backup.
Before he was through he shot his dog
as well mistaking it for a sixth cow
in the powder smoke and diesel fumes.
And he put one for good measure
into the police car radiator though
he didn't mean to do it but what
the hell when the trigger finger gets
going it's hard to stop the damn twitch
in time he was heard to say later.

While they were using the tractor
to drag the dead cows off the highway
the wife came out in her little Japanese car
and brought him a slice of rhubarb pie.
It made all the difference in a hard day.
He grew whimsical about the experience
noting the expensive meat hulks piled up
like a neat stack of cordwood in the ditch.
The cop eating his piece of pie a la mode
shrugged his ample shoulders when his backup
squad arrived wearing riot gear.

WITHOUT DOUBT

The direction you take
into the wild country
ragged wind, big mud
drying up hard as concrete
at different times of year
eyes fill with a sandy vision
grit in the mainstream
the breeze takes you apart
lifting your hair on a gust
grabbing at baggy pants
long coat tail flapping
like a sail on a small boat

Within a few hours
completely becalmed
on an ocean of bent grass
under a withering sun
cries of crows berate
the omnipresent silence
moving along like sentences
composed of black words
written on the faint hills
in a style of primitive
handwriting authorised
by the sprawl of nature

At last the voice of water
in a small clear creek
comes out of the ground
running practically nowhere
back into the earth
beginning and end
in one small trickery
a transparent green frog
with black jig head eyes
rubbery white legs
with a long slow kick
sinks to the bottom

INVISIBLE NIGHT

there goes black night out the window
on the highway to everywhere
now travelling blind into notions
about velocity and likelihood of impact

white cane at the steering wheel taps
on the gas pedal whistling Beethoven
in the darkness no birds to watch fly by
or horizon to imagine a future destination

the odd yard light situated here or there
helping to create an ethereal visibility
hysterical twin sirens in the distance
take a long time coming forward

Washed out neon in the morning sun like a fish out of water
A swift silence follows the odd vehicle travelling through town
there are no people on the sidewalks as the crows fly up
from the main intersection when the light changes to green
they know they have enough time to get out of the way
They flutter back on the pavement behind the back window
as if to claim the emptiness that will soon be filled by traffic
going to work or moving down the highway to the next place
taking the black spaces with them from under the motel beds
There is no reason to leave them behind without a reason
Water from their morning showers trickles into the ground

A smoking cigarette butt left behind in an asphalt parking lot
last memory like a gob of spit left on a motel bathroom mirror
Don't ask me why certain people want to be remembered
or why those intelligent birds want to play in that intersection
Soon enough it's all a minor memory of washed out colour
that ruled the night in magic illustrations of neon splendour
Even the bristling prairie stars were put in the background
by the pulse of electronic graffiti owning complete darkness
Life in meaning only partially told before it answers back
laughing bravely at the stranger elements of blind faith
Who'll be there tomorrow or the next day waiting for me

LORRAINE FALLS MAINLY ON THE PLAIN

There was something about her voice
shredding onions in the winter gloom
while outside the warmed up kitchen
window ice fog drifted into the bare trees
The sight of her in the yard curdled milk,
paralysed laying hens, frightened the dog
into moving over to the neighbour's house.

She put strawberry birthmarks on the faces
of the friendships she managed to destroy
there were plenty of those from childhood on
including siblings who went to other continents;
More than pungent onions made her cry
the weevils that showed up in her flour bin
the bad wallpaper half stuck on the hallway.

When she went out to the garden the bees left,
grass stopped growing, flowers aborted
a number of pickets dropped off the fence
the cement sidewalk cracked like a mirror
the bright sun became obscured by hail.
While I watched birds swimming in the sky
I heard the cocker spaniel call my name.

THE NATURAL HISTORY OF THE STRIPED SKUNK*

(Latin name, *Mephitis mephitis* means
"terrible smell, terrible smell")

The Striped skunk waddles down the dusty
road, half eaten beetle in it's ratty mouth
beady eyes focus six inches in front of its face
shakes it's busy black and white tail
a trophy that must be obeyed at all times
I get down to look at its tracks in the sand
"Undulating smooth as a Japanese brushstroke.
A perfect shadow of the endearing waddle."
"Skunks roll caterpillars on the ground
to remove the hairs before eating them."

The Striped skunk, about the size of a house cat."
Black body with a white stripe along each side."
"Name in French Mouffette Rayée."
"Born blind with fur in a skunkly pattern."
"By eight days, the young can emit musk."
"While similar, every stripe pattern is unique."
"The Striped skunk is generally nocturnal.
In winter month diurnal on overcast days."
"Placid and sluggish; they hiss, growl, squeal and coo."
"Never approach an overly friendly skunk."

"Young skunks are more likely to spray
than more experienced skunks."
"A skunk can discharge musk 12 feet
with good accuracy. On a windy day,
spray may reach 18 feet downwind."
"Expelled as a fine mist or as droplets.

Can carry one kilometre in the breeze."
"Skunk's white stripes point to the area
where it fires its foul-smelling spray
Two large musk glands at the base of the tail,
a visual reminder to any animal or foe."

"Contrary to popular myth, cannot spray
over its back. Stands on its front feet, arches
its back to direct the stream over its head."
"Fetid, oily, yellowish musk, produced in anal
glands which hold about a tablespoon of liquid."
"A striped skunk can shoot five to eight times
before it has to reload, which takes about a week."

"A group of skunks together,
are called a 'surfeit' of skunks."
"Aware of the repulsiveness of its own
odour — skunk will not spray in its den."
"The *crepuscular* skunk begins searching
for food at dawn and dusk. Polygamous males
defend harems of females. When pregnant
they drive the male away and live communally."
"Skunks are a primary predator of the honeybee."

"Every year thousands of skunks are killed
for their pelts, which are worth about 2 dollars."
"Large fur farms sell surplus skunks to pet stores."
"The skunk is not molested by many animals."
"The Great Horned Owl, its major predator,
attacking from above has no sense of smell."

Note the words of a local woman;
"I love the fresh smell of skunk.
It reminds me of all the wild things
still living in my neighbourhood."
or the words of the naturalist
who proselytised on the skunk;
"Dogs generally get into trouble
because like many people they don't
seem to know when to back down."

---

*a found poem made from various quotations by skunk experts

BITTER SWEET

Love my jar of baby pickles
full of sunshine and summer
they taste of iron water
rushing into sandy earth
under flush cucumber leaves

Blackbird's eccentric song
travels into the window's glass
on a long thread of electricity
birds scattered in the garden
balance on tall sweet-corn stalks

I leave them in the ground all winter
(when the black January nights float
down from the Milky Way)
to hear the paper rustle in the wind

Nothing reminds me so much
of summer as devouring small
crunchy dills and pickled garlic

DRYLAND

In the Chinese/Canadian cafe
arid voices in low conversation
Nobody talks much to strangers
except about the weather

Unless you're born here
you'll always be a stranger
Waiting on elsewhere

You will never be asked why
They already know you're leaving
when you arrive. Never to return

In a small graveyard
a few family names repeat
in a sequence of straight rows
Strangers die other places

MOOSE RACK ON THE HIGHWAY AT HANLEY

What hit you, maybe a rogue locomotive
disguised as a freight truck with a tandem
and a pup swaying dangerously behind
on a full moon night in the semi wilderness
or some kind of ancient space vehicle
accelerating at twice the speed of sound

1400 hundred pounds of red meat
wrapped in coarse haired black hide
advertised on a fifty foot banner of blood
Do you want that salted or cured in a smoker?
the rack twisted into a rocking chair shape
on the cold hard surface of the road

Nobody left a note pinned on its shoulder;
"Sorry happened to be approaching warp drive
unusual livestock wandered onto the tarmac
came up a big shadow on the invisible screen
felt like we ran over a small mountain
have you found our muffler and exhaust pipe?"

The Indian bone shaker looked at the remains
nothing makeable from these tortured palms
they've seen better days on a living moose
before they were splintered and twisted
the moose nose looks silly as it always does
shrivelling up on the dead animal side of the road

   Allan Safarik

ROCK UPON A HARD PLACE

Scrabble ground of rocky futility
nothing breaks here, everything
endures beyond the thin shade

nothing changes but change itself
an unknown star coming into range
a grain of sand located in the desert

empty eye holes fill up with dirt
bone chips flake as easily as flint
tumble weeds pick up the slack

a few boulders scattered by time
loquacious in the arid landscape
from ten million years of silence

THE EMPTY HEN HOUSE

In the dark room
scarce light
barely grimaces
at the pool balls
gathered like eggs
in the side pockets
an ancient rooster
drags his ass over
a nearly bald piss
coloured carpet

Two old boys
drink Pil
the worn out
hickory cues
are all garbage
the leaky urinals
in the mensroom
barely hang on
to decrepit walls

The hot dogs
are unusually bad
with stale buns
despicable meat
a few inebriated
fancy chickens
might liven
up the joint

Exit sign winks
a lovely smile
at your leavings
an empty glass
a juke box full
of sad songs

GRUMBLE HAT

"What do want to argue about today?"
Sal asked when Lamont walked
through the front door beneath
his ten gallon Smithbuilt jammed
on a shiny bald head full of vitriol
about the nation and its inhabitants
"Steak sandwich hold the salad."

Soldier boys in the front window
in civvies just back from Kandahar
said you couldn't tell the good ones
from the bad and the indifferent
"Guess they all look pretty much alike
when they blow up in the noon heat."
Lamont said sucking his toothpick

"Do you want gravy with that?"Sal asked.
"Gravy? that's a hard question to answer
without thinking about it for a while like
choosing between white or brown toast.
City folk look and sound the same to me
'specially the woman that set their teeth
and talk like Mickey Mouse on crack.

They don't know which end's up on a beef
or how to go about butchering a hog
and they let their cat live in the house."
Lamont chimed pouring the coal
to the bottom of the catsup bottle
"Bet the donkeys in Afghanistan have
aching backs and short memories."

ESTEVAN

We drove down to the border
for a look across at North Dakota
We wanted to see the American
border guard with the mirror
on his shoe walking stiff legged
poking his cowboy boot toe
under each rusted chassis
looking for tiny Arabs
scrunched into rusty places
under the muffler

Everyday they paraded
the canine core
Dogs trained to sniff
every hole in the body
I watch one straining at the leash
pull his handler
into the trunk of a new car
Now he's trying to hump
the Asian couple
in the back seat

If the dog pointed
his boner in my direction
and started to get excited
trying to screw me
for smuggling msg
I'd have to throw up
the load of high grade
Chinese food
I'm wearing around
my padded midsection

We walk by on
the Canadian side
knowing the guilty smell
of our being permeates
the arid country
Bush's Rangers, baby faces
set in stone masks
poised to nab us
even if we dare attempt
to cross the border
in our imaginations

We wear innocence
like cheap cologne
the odour of sanctimonious
Canadian unleashed
without ardour or anger
essence of dismay
The dog, sensing
the weight of our
disobedient souls
snarls, hurling himself
against the wire fence

HOAR FROST ON HALLOWEEN

Moonlight ceases in the conquest of turmoil
smoky clouds steadily pile in from the west
the lunar body goes out like the bulb in the hall
before I climb into the down covered bed
decades old winter etched window glass rattles

a reminder voice remembers the bones
of the past in rows marked by tombstones
heavy with the burden of time and loneliness
in the brown grassy cemetery across town
a single fox wanders in brittle ditch weed

searching for the scent of a familiar vixen
a white owl muffles the air with padded wings
dropping down from a power pole catches
a meal of blood that it will tear asunder
yet, nothing in the stillness but a cough

or an isolated murmur to define the silence
the night runs by without us, as if sleep
makes everything unreal and temporary
until another smouldering lunar night
comes to obscure the weariness of the fall

slaughtered colours slide into hard ground
wind bends saplings into twisted spears
biting cold stiffens the grip of icy fingers
driven beneath the gleaned surface
beauty of hoar frost marks the occasion

WEYBURN

Nearly every window in all the stately homes
black and empty enveloping sleepers
the sound of snoring shatters crystal air
Nothing moving but me down one way streets
All the traffic lights in town flashing yellow
I drove back out to the highway
crusted with black ice and rutted tracks
the all night ninja in me, really a pacifist
with an overactive imagination

Still, I couldn't find your house number
decide to stop and have a full breakfast
imagine my shock when your sleepy
face turns up staring at me over a plate
of fried eggs and link sausages
Later in the frozen parking lot
a pterodactyl swooped down
over town on stretched leather wings
Beak snapping at the wooden flag pole

This might be some kind of local tourist trick
A large meat eating flying dinosaur
soaring about at 6 am at twenty-five below zero
looking for something soft and fuzzy to eat
This isn't unusual for Saskatchewan
only the fact it isn't wearing a saddle

DRIFTER

Got off the bus
checked into the motel
seven weeks ago
Living on grilled cheese
sound of it spattering on the grill
Gallons of highway coffee
a worn-out magazine rack
radical colour on the motel TV

Waiting, everybody
thought, for what?
Not much for random conversation
Could be waiting on a trucker
or a mysterious car full of strangers
Suppose there's the possibility
of a woman arriving mysteriously
and maybe a jealous husband

Not really the partying type
The new Ukrainian waitress,
falling fast like a fall flower
under the skinny sun
knocked over the candle
in the night of shadowy pictures
burning the acid yellow carpet
Green and blue tattoos
slightly out-of-focus
under artificial light

Next morning a flock
of black and white geese
walked on the swathes
in the field behind the motel
He got back on the bus
Bitter prairie wind yapping
down the highway
a half frozen dog
licked the window panes

WHEN IT SEEMED UNLIKELY

A sudden banging on the front door,
the startled dog convulsing on the rug
he hates surprises and loud noises
figuring, I'm sure that his world
might be coming to an end
from the thumping fist
on the impressive oak door

it was only a pip-squeak
in a black suit preaching
the word of God by rote

(The dog soon calmed down
quickly growing uninterested
dragging his meaty thigh bone
of venison under the coffee table)

Perspiration on his upper lip
glistened a hydrogen peroxide
rainbow in the sunlight
as he explained his mission
in Vietnam and his zeal
to travel into the Asian jungle
with a backpack full of bibles

while sampling a cuisine
stamped with the imprimatur
of Imperial French culture

On a cold winter morning
I shot the dog's dinner right
through the head and dragged it
a long way across a frozen field

BLUE HOUSE WINDOWS

A few bruised words arguing
outside fell down in agony
Burying themselves in dirty
midnight snow banks
on the shrouded street

What's dark and blurry
in the startled sleepy eye?
Night shifts into morning
cold ideas stirred in ashes
regain the raw light

IN THE DARK

A billion white stars
on top of the northern plains
wind here has mettle
cold bites into the bone
the landscape dies down
freezes hard as a brick
eight feet underground

When the dog is barking
and the elm tree beside
the house scratches boldly
at the window desperate
to come in from the cold
do you think I bother
getting up to investigate
a shot in the dark?

No I stay in my bed
cover up to my ears
with my feet resting
on the hot water bottle
a Louisville Slugger handy
behind the bedroom door
thinking me clairvoyant
you wake me
wondering what
the noise is about

I turn over and go
back into deep sleep
after yelling shutup
at the hoarse dog
who is carrying on

running up down
under the yard lights
as if he's seen a ghost
and maybe he has

I'll wait until morning's
shabby light invades
the edges of the blinds
to find out who shot what
knowing most likely
there's nothing to it

THE GREEN GRASS OF WINTER

Wind scratches at God's eye
with a branch twisted out of shape
the tree poses like a crucified man
nailed into a corner of the tin roof

At dawn the displayed body
warmed by a white cover of frost
smoulders in the lightly coloured sky
until it swallows a frozen stone

When cold light decides to leave
nothing left but shivering stars
scimitar moon rising in the east
to define the picture of darkness

IN THE WHITE FOREST

"When did you go down to the river?"
What voice plaintively called
you further and further out on
the surface of wind honed ice?
Burning a red mark against one
cheek as you slid on your face
down around the first bend
How did you pass through
the white forest without leaving
a shadow of doubt, something
bruised or temporarily altered?

Not one transient memory
about endless time out of place
Mind wanders in a trance
travelling over open country
on a prayer and a wing
Words have no power until
the spirit releases them in short
bursts to wake up the wilderness
No tracks to anywhere
only pristine snowy fields
white trees stiff as wire brushes

NEWS OF THE WORLD

Vacant windows stare
out at dark shadows
beside a snowy field
saw you dig out your car
exhaust whipped away by
a forehead scaring wind

No birds in early morning
winter sky just the tracks
of some animal that walked
across the immaculate surface
sun slowly coming up deepens
the profound visual contrast
transparent invisibility
ignited by ethereal light
pours through the glass

Black trees stand together
along edges in every direction
outlining limits of structure
nothing new to report
eternity still going on here
and the breath taking silence

II. FURTHER NOTES

WHERE I SHOULD NOT BE KNOCKING

Walk away from the awful truth I should not be talking
Strangers go by oblivious to the drifting conversation
Saw you hanging in the back of the church balcony
Pretended I could not see through stained glass

When the voice of the priest lifted up into the rafters
The butcher went forth with his wife for communion
There is no life without God he said wiping his mouth
On the back of his sleeve, a new jacket I believe

Hung on him like a badly formed sack in gabardine
Came to the light in the middle of something new
Now the saddest day of all passes by in full flight
Gone down the long thirsty roadway forgotten

EASTER RAIN

Cloud image man in a Christly pose

before a flock of raging sinners in a temple

A ship passing through a vast wave of souls

casts a net into the sea and takes a huge haul

of long haired fishy creatures with human heads

On the horizon a bristling army marches

against thunderheads in the eastern sky

Warm rain slakes unbroken thirsty fields

blood falls drop by drop in the fickle desert

until an unbloody deluge erases the imaginary

EXPLICIT UNIVERSE

I'd take you travelling to the valley of hope
if I had a peashooter, a length of rope
with maybe one pretty owl decoy
and an ashtray to hold the shooting stars
you bring all the ice you can carry
should we come across a bleeding angel
and a shotgun in case the Devil shows

Never can tell what you'll find in the desert
a seed, maybe the inside of a sea shell
the remains of a time stressed skull
or the white birds never touching down
on sandy waves that never lap a shore
the moon comes up like a cheap lantern
somebody purchased from a garage sale

THE SHRINKAGE

Made the mistake
of telling my father
about my dead mother
visiting my dreams.
He got upset because
she hadn't come to him.

"Might as well have
given the fox the keys
to the hen-house,"
the shrink advised;
"and left him a recipe
for fried chicken."

THE FALSE MESSIAH

A lot of solace in the words
most people thought heading
down the wide stairs waiting
around for the hearse to pull out
from the ignored 5 min loading
zone in front of the steep spire
seeming to reside in the clouds.

The face in the coffin serene
as if peacefully asleep even
when thunder banged the sky
with enthusiasm for salvation.
Jagged lightning trees filled
the stained glass with the beauty
of the crucifixion illuminated.

God's on our side the obvious
message repeated in the litany
before the bemused smile
from the immaculately coifed
spectator in the new suit
below the vaulted ceiling.
I prayed for him to rise up
right then and there to lead us

To the promised rooms in heaven.
Doubt ran like the small brown
mouse along the baseboards
down under the wooden floor
into the church basement
just in time to get into the bowl
of unattended potato salad

     Allan Safarik

along with pickles, cheese,
slices of ham and bologna
awaiting the mourners.
Later, the bejewelled
arthritic knuckles
of old ladies ladled
out the canned soup.

AQUARIUM FOLK

The guppy coffee drinkers have crowded in
Around the tables closest to the windows
The piranha still circling the entire room
Looking for something to get mad about
The gold fish have everything to lose

Locked in group prayer across the way
If he shows colour and zips off their fins
They'll be big eyed golden teardrops
Bouncing on the sandy bottom minus
Essential frilly music hall accoutrements

Way down in a far corner of the glass box
In the working stiff section of the universe
The algae eater's busy cramming wads
Of toilet paper in his several shaving wounds
So he can look sharp for the rest of the day

THE PATRON

A child made a drawing of his grandpa
who hated it and threw it in the garbage
admonishing it as a dishonest picture
that might as well be destroyed

Twenty years later the little boy
long grown out of his childish skin
executed a thousand drawings based
on the one he made as a child

The inspiration his grandpa debased
sharpened the clarity of his vision
however, none of the drawings
equalled the quality of the original

LICKING THE WOLF'S CHOPS

For once I want to read a story
about a sheep screwing a wolf
rather than the other way around.
The mother sheep saying to the lambs
"Well look at this well screwed wolf
if we weren't strict vegetarians
we'd have this fine fellow for dinner"
while the daddy sheep does knee
bends to emphasis his conditioning
in front of the tall hallway mirror

Now the vigilante sheep went out
in the bush and hunted the wolves
on their own territory pissing on
every second rock just like wolves
do and circling the pack with wild
crazy eyes like bikers on speed
every sheep gets a new fur hat
and wolf tail to put on their bicycle
when they ride proudly around in
the fresh air in the spring pasture

THE LAST VISITOR

A sweltering afternoon in mid-July
perennial flowers smiled at the sun
staying too long above the house
until the warped shingles squirmed
and the chimney screamed for relief
as if it were being tickled to death

When it stopped it had sore bricks
The glass that let in the sharp light
blinded the old dog for so long
his image became semi-permanent
He took forever to come down
the sidewalk to lick my offered hand

before he went back to lay down
in the shade under the crab apple tree
The window needed darkness to come
in and address the question of balance
Staying up all night at attention
on the wall beside the back door

CRAZY FOX COMES TO TOWN

The slick red fox chasing a rabbit
into Mrs Pendleman's garden
never forgot the lesson he got
when she busted him in the groin
with a size twelve steel rake
he went and hid in the rhubarb
waiting for a crippled rodent

finally, he recovered enough
to drag himself down on 1 st Street
where a bunch of kids on the corner
playing with matches accidentally
set his well endowed tail on fire
then put it out with oven mitts
filled with applauding hands

dipping it into a can of grease
behind old Bill's two car garage.
Pretty soon he had one paw
in a sling and another in a trap
while the back two legs jockeyed
for position out of the rain
dancing like Fred Astaire

a teacher at the local school
asked the kids what this taught
them about wildlife and mankind
"Two parts of the same thing
or the same old thing twice"
the first answer that made
any sense to casual thinkers.

Yet, there were no foxes
growing in the town's gardens
no matter how hard the locals
tried to cultivate them under
the mulch away from the heat
of summer that brought on
that infestation of rabbits.

in memory of Czeslaw Milosz

Where time meets the horizon

Death drives the yellow taxi every night at midnight

There are lights in all the windows

A stone in the alley for every handshake

Cool shadows hug limestone walls

People here invisible until darkness uncovers them

History is the story of repetition repeated

The blood of martyrs quenches fire storms

It has never rained cats and frogs in Hong Kong

The world of meditation will never run short of vegetation

But look how the fog lingers over yonder hills

There's always a good reason for remaining silent

The pace of life around here weighs a man down

Shark faces smile in the subway car aquarium

A glass of whisky per day keeps the bile fit

The bath tub overflows into the living room below

Graffiti is a text/image addressed to God

A bloke with big knuckles comes to the front door

A Nat King Cole record is skipping on the turn table

Fish in the rooftop gutters are swimming upstream

I would be happy to share tricks for memorising

Everyday another UFO lands in New York City

Hello there's still time to say good-bye

Blue light finds its way into secret hiding places

Look for a chicken bone in a miserable throat

Dawn brings blackmailers into the tree tops

A chunky gold ring swallowed with a piece of wonder bread

No choice but to pick up and move to a new locale

Sand in a hour glass or in a pair of shoes?

The eternal voice of spring, a few tender shoots

Nobody of that name living at this address

Winds of change blow softly into ears of the stubborn

Who can say when the clock hands will stop moving?

The five senses, a beautiful reward for living

A black dog showed up when required

The night train pulls through town on jangling wheels

Thoughts and words reveal detailed maps of the interior

A fence post pounded into earth outlasts many friendships

There is a voice within the voice behind the eyes

Who can stand staring into the sun's eternal glare?

Church pews polished by decades of shiny pants

White flowers announce the end of the conscious world

Sleepers who dream get charged by the minute

So much depends on loose tin banging in the wind

THE SUMMONING

Looking at the worn out photos
of peasant farmers from an earlier era
in a country whose name and borders
have changed often in dividing times
here are the isolated, serious faces
of the unhappy few who were caught
by the camera before they were ready to smile
they look almost ghostly as the pale throat
of wind pulls curtains out the open window

The three men all wear mud covered boots
the woman holds a toddler close to her breast
two teenagers stand in the background
looking alienated, bored out of their skulls
The old man without any front teeth
holds up the slack body of a dead rabbit
a limber black and white dog below sniffs
at the hind legs and the dangling feet
there are drops of blood on his shirtfront

It was the last photo ever taken of them
although the dog lived ten more years
dying of old age on gimpy hindquarters
in a dog house behind a neighbour's barn
unlike the others who suffered the same fate
as the fat rabbit they feasted lovingly upon
when lead slugs took them down in the grass
the song of the shovel buried them quickly
under the undulating carpet of the pasture

     Allan Safarik

THE MANY LEGGED BUG

What dreams I carry down the watery valley of blue nirvana
the dentist never stopped pumping in the Novocain until
I was dancing and singing like Marvin Gaye on hyper reality
when the whole chorus cut in drowning out my moving lips

Watched in the mirror as all my legs moved one by one
down the long slippery field of images and reflections
elementary locomotion in syncopated harmony
an organic biology like Xerxes's army at Thermophylae

Marching over the landscape like a many legged bug
I flew away on the smoky wings of a marsh grass fire
that threatened to turn all the blue mountains white
while the boggy blooded sun fell hard on the horizon

Woke up suddenly still in a dream in a ultra white room
robes on my body white as snow and outlined in blue
as the coldest winters etched in time slowly passed by
the many legged bug wandered into the other place

Stone cold dead amongst discarded whiskers left
in the porcelain sink beside the carved ivory wall
a small battle helmet with enough loafers on each side
to open a fashionable shoe store in a trendy loft in Soho

HEAT STALKS THE THIRSTY SAND

Watery walls fall in a mirage
above screaming heat waves
eyes groaning in piercing light
weep like upset children
who have gone on too long
without taking a breath
inertia flicks ugly beetles
making seed pod rattling
leaps across the beaten sand
until one lands upside down
on a sizzling frying pan rock
same spotted undercarriage
painted on Queen Victoria's
lacquered coronation coach
many legs twizzle at the sun

Later a bold face comes up
on edge a smiling Buddha
wearing an odd pair of shoes
with long singing tongues
an old ship wrecked sailor
to hang out with shadowy
figures at the debutantes' ball
smooth aura of moonlight
a well to mime the drop
dead beauty of an insect star
crawling desperately along
the trail of the Beehive Cluster
measurements by hour glass
vivid dream of black ice
in an obsidian eternity

OUT LATE

The door's open wide
the radio's playing
there's a half cooked chop
in the frying pan
nobody's home

How can I be impatient?
falling rain rusting
wrought iron railings
on the front porch
right before my eye

TELL YOU WHAT

Says Ted the house painter
"I'll give you ten to one odds
the moon doesn't come out tonight."
Why would I make such a stupid bet
I thought putting my ten down
Waited on my back looking up

at the sky from a reposing position
he was right no moon to see
or much of a night to remember
Fell asleep in the chaise lounge
on the back porch woke-up
with the sun torturing the side

of my face that's talking with you
a red bug with crinkly back legs
hid in the hair on my arm
Scared him off with a close-up
of my big snorting nostrils
"Tell you what," I said to Ted

"I'll give you even money
that bug had its way with me."
"How can you prove it?" he asked.
"Didn't have to tell him but I did."

GRAVESIDE SINNER

God broke the heart of an astonished newby
who didn't have enough strength to lift his end
he found religion too big a pill to swallow
so he bit it in two and became half a sinner

So much light passes through the naked eye
there's no time to remember tomorrow
suddenly youngish hands are old and fragile
the ragged voice cannot find the words

There's glory in life and death done well
like the dance of thieves beside the loot
the hole opens, only the weight of darkness
escapes, before the shovel bites the dust

DOING RESEARCH INTO THE FUTURE I SAW
THE DYING LIGHT OF MY IMAGE WITHERING
IN A NOT YET COMPLETELY DARK PLACE

When at last you know where you belong
you've weathered a few thousand
pissing down storms on the streets
Walked another thousand miles
in the same worthless pair of shoes
without carrying an umbrella
Made the same pitiful speech
so many times you have the memorised
words handed out on printed sheets
for the choir singing in the background

Life a one way window looking in at the end
Breaking into sealed memory cells like a thief
maybe it's a last attempt to warm up the soul
before it's forced to flutter off to a new locale
in another less worldly dimension
Packed up a lifetime of work in half a dozen
cardboard boxes left behind in the back
of a borrowed pickup truck that got stolen
Well taken care of books find a new home
in an environmentally friendly incinerator
Now that computers own the world
the printed word falls into disuse
until the computer age comes to an end
and knowledge has to be reinvented

Time wears the paint from pictures
on cracked faded living room walls
like makeup fades on a dummy
That's my face in the disappearing light
a pale moon hiding in a corner of the sky
Flowers grow tall and thin in the meadow
to see above the wall of scraggily weeds
Even the casual bird flying by knows that
Until darkness closes down and says
no to everything snuffing out the light

TO CATCH THE LIGHT

Dawn came pointedly in through the attic window
where dust mites ruled the world for over a century
I noticed the glint when I arrived home at dawn
thinking about light passing into that dusty space
every morning while in rooms below sleepers awake
"Why do you always bring up mundane obscure things?"
you stated firmly when we came inside from the car

They often come with the territory I inhabit
Looking up and watching black birds build a nest
in the chimney rising up in the middle of the roof
Now we have borders, maybe we can charge rent
or go out at night gathering planets in a picnic basket
catch moonlight in a barrel and sell it to sailors
although it's a thousand miles to the West Coast

Rabbits on the long gravel driveway come out
at night and light the roadway with flashlight eyes
The shuffling black and white spotted polecat
leaves his stink shimmering on the newly cut lawn
We wander looking for new celestial openings
a falling star or wayward satellite we can salvage
for scrap or turn into an unusual garden ornament

THE HIRED MAN

You can't sleep too often in the same bed
unless you bring flowers and compliments
The country calling through the window
for you to leave this place now and save
yourself from falling head over heels
in love with the redheaded woman
who wants your soul to settle down
in her garden, in her ample bed
Her breasts are an exaggerated
landscape that needs containment
the big trees are overgrown in need
of pruning and there is no ladder
Do you need another hint about
the bus schedule in the morning?

If you miss it you are doomed
to stay here for the rest of your life
digging potatoes in the early fall.
No law says you have to stay around
unless you've lost your mind and wish
to make up a lie about your itchy feet
and the business you have to tend to
in the rocky country by the seacoast.
She'll know you're lying and she's ready
to give you the full treatment in stereo
There's no way out unless you kill
the white chickens and pluck them
well and cool them in cold water
until the heat has ceased to burn
the bones black and render the flesh

FROM HER POINT OF VIEW

Give me a man with scars
any time over a smooth talker
I trace my fingers over them
making a map of recreation
the glib man is out the door
dragging his baggage behind
like the wag on the dog's tail
his calluses are on his tongue

The rough man has no time
for any form of conversation
especially at dinner time
he's as silent as the tall peas
growing in rows in the garden
his strong sandpaper hands
leave no doubt about where
he's been on my pretty skin

DREAM IN THE GARDEN

In my dream I was sewing my nose
back into the middle of my face
with stout black thread and a large
needle that I pulled through the skin
with a red handled pair of needle nose pliers
trying to keep in the centre somewhat
in harmony with my slanted brown eyes
and not falling into my mouth

Kept the stitches down to a small size
so it didn't look like a railway track
waiting for a train to pass this way
and damn if I didn't come up short
and accidentally sew my thumb
clumsily to one side of an eyelid
while I was pinching things in place
with a handful of grasping fingers

The other hand had to carefully
snip the line and rethread the needle
which I had trouble doing
since I had no nose in place to hold
the wire frame of my glasses
which kept fogging up big time
and kept me from having even
a vague look at the end result

It appeared to me in the mirror
that my thumb looked better
masquerading as my nose
than my nose looked being a nose
A rose by any other name
(even if sewn by stout black thread
onto a stem with a couple of leaves)
could never be mistaken for a thumb

CONSIDER THE DREAM OF POSSIBLE MEMORIES

The threat of rain rattled the leaves so we went back inside
She sat by the door, I perched by the hearth, stirring the fire
It started to rain harder, splattering the metal roof
The lake turned as grey as the travelling sky,
"Maybe he's not coming," she said, lighting a candle
Giving me the look that buckled my legs at the knees
"After all we've done for him he has no choice,"
I answered, pouring the water from the bucket
into the blackened kettle on the rough slate

A car crawled up the long gravel hill but passed by
while we sat holding our breath in the gloom
"Not him, I guess, or he's having second thoughts
about stopping without having a look."
"No," she said. "He's not the back door type."
I sat in silence watching out the window for headlights
Moving over she leaned her head on my shoulder
"There's nothing I wouldn't do for you,"
barely touching the flesh on my forearm

"You say that now, but what's the point."
I went around and started pulling down the shades
It was nearly dark, raining in windy torrents
like fingers drumming against the side of a tin cup
I watched the water leaking down the chimney stones
She sat in the corner biting her lip in a thoughtful pose
projecting a shadow puppet on the wide cedar planks
"Since we met I smell permanently like bedroom."

We both heard the sound of wheels grinding on gravel
She moved quickly to the other side of the cabin
I opened the door, the coldness of the wind rushed in
"Where is he?" she screamed, looking out at the darkness

I put my hand on her waist, she didn't seem to notice
"It's a joke." she said, wiping my arm away
"He's playing a joke." I went out and looked around
"Must be hearing things." The rain seemed to be letting up

Headlights penetrated the wall of night
She ran out to the road waving her lovely arms
but the car splashed by, heading east in a hurry
"Damn it! Damn it!" she said, "he's not coming!"
I could smell the fire, the kettle had boiled dry
We both knew she was right. I looked at the tears
in her eyes, wondering for a few seconds, if she'd cry
that hard for me but I already knew the answer

BLACK LETTER DAY

This Times Roman reading has got to stop
On the subway on the highway on the rooftop
In bed in the bathtub on the porcelain backstop

Headlines crawl like ants across white sand
Nuclear accidents have almost paralysed Japan
These are things that whales can understand

Choir boys sing a capella in the starry dark
You run the dog around the bushes in the park
The hooker on the corner engages another mark

Read all about it in the early morning news
Where harping critics hock pessimistic views
About who and what have caused eternal blues

While the human condition sinks further into dust
Read on page six about the pop singer's child lust
And the thieving praying politicians lack of trust

Do you see the ink smudged on my fingers
The stain from so many exaggerations linger
I take no solace or joy from words that injure

Can you see my pitiful face through the window
Transparent as the next man I breath in indigo
While the blood in my lungs does the fandango

Almost dried up and blew my aching heart away
Disappeared across the plains vanishing yesterday
Lost and found in a daze on a dusty road in May

Remember all your friends to your lost beauty
Left behind and long forgotten I did my duty
Buried wilted flowers and found another cutie

The river of sorrow ran away in an empty street
Woke up in time to avoid the wrath of stifling heat
No other way to escape becoming mindless meat

Put another coat of paint on the walls of fate
Managed to get time to stay around and wait
In case the muse was lingering by the open gate

That's me in wrinkles and grey hair in the corner
Turned old and tired before I knew the coroner
Would find me one day in a draughty corridor

Enough of me left behind on paper to make a fire
That will burn all night fuelled by an old black tire
Greeting the sun on the hill beside my funeral pyre

DAY OF RECKONING

Sunday afternoon reading the re-
read newspaper one more time
a fly touches down on the dining room
table I reach to slap with the swatter
something inside goes wrong
for a minute or two I am wobbly
but it passes into the energy of the day
a sudden prolonged twinge to remind
me to take a long slow drink of water

The fly laughs at me in its deep
bass voice when it lands on my head
trying to buzz its way in through my ear
"Have you ever tasted fly?" it asks
in metaphorical language crawling
in the slippery puddles of sweat
sticking to my clammy skin
"No I can't say I have intentionally
swallowed a bristling blue bottle

I once sucked in a honey bee
while running full bore down
a straightaway on a cinder track
coughing up its various sections
like a parts dealer trying to put
the metaphysics back in place
a pair of perfectly intact wings
spat into the palm of my hand
stinger plucked from my tongue"

FLIGHT INTO THE DESERT

Do not smile, my friends! a handkerchief, as those familiar
with the fate of Shakespeare's gentle Desdemona know,
is no trivial affair. A handkerchief is at once the most alluring
and yet the most fatal web that ever came from the loom

In beauty's hand it leads us on to love and folly; in that of the
captain of the file its fall means death by the swiftly flying bullet;
in that of the headsman its wave means blood and sawdust
a covered basket and a headless corse

— found in the prose of Frank Triplett
(corse, archaic var. of corpse)

Cold night, when the ice cube stars came out
they rattled about like dice in a big cup
In the morning hiking across purple sand hills
Dust puts all tortured scrubby bewildered
things out of their ever loving misery
Take the twisted wire bushes and the rebar trees
Gleaming steel wool in the early morning desert
I rolled a fat herbal cigarette in a thin paper
counted deer chewing on dry thorny plants
watched an eagle spin off the edge of time

"When did you come upon our trail?" he asked,
lowering his eyes, the half-hidden-part
of him offering a muted threat from
the shadowy background and an attitude that said
if I blow up we're both going to the after world
What I'm carrying in this rolled up blanket
heavy enough to cause an international incident
Figure it could be anything, maybe a portable
laser, a nuclear salami or a simple switch blade
Bad sign when there's no acoustic guitar

Famous Roadkill   97

hanging by a beaded strap on the backpack
or God's eye to decorate the omnipotent universe

The woman with him moved to the small fire
sat down and pulled the cork from a whisky bottle
This is where we spent the winter, she said
Showing me pictures of the probe to Mars
Motels are all the same, where ever you go
I thought out loud as she winked at me through
cheap plastic sunglasses and strawberry lip gloss
She said they spent all their money on the slots
I moved on, left them in the dry gulch bottom
drinking red wine from a tall green bottle
Later in the afternoon when it got really hot
I heard it smash behind me on the rocky path

When I stopped on the trail for lunch he came out
of the scrubby underbrush and asked for a spliff
He held his arms wide apart, said he wasn't armed
but I could see the bulge under his waistband
I gave him my last can of Chef Boyardi spaghetti
Soon meatballs were frying under the scalding sun
"Too bad you couldn't shoot a gopher or two
or a snake for supplementary meat in the frying pan"
I offered weakly in an attempt to disarm his cunning smile
But the silence and the yellow flecks in his blue eyes
said all there was to know about his clinical condition
He had eaten all the cold death he was going to eat

Something changed him, she said, in her breathless
way, maybe it was the bird pecking the eyes
from the living animal as it thrashed in the grass
or something tangible from his sordid past
The foster parents bamboo cane discipline
Breathing in the asbestos in those awful schools

The vd he got in the back seat of the Chevrolet
The bad wallpaper in all the halfway houses
or that last concussion when bikers collected his scalp
on the end of heavily wrapped hickory pool cue
for the white powder that dribbled away in his spit

Is this man already dead wandering in the desert
with his winsome companion or am I seeing things?
The mirage opens again inside my mind I see
a turquoise lake surrounded by white dunes
I feel the bullet entering the back of my head
Eyes straight ahead see a full frame of blue air fly apart,
Smell of acrid powder and the sound
ricocheting into my pelvis and down
my left leg into the sandy ground while my eyes
are bobbing corks in the sea of blood

No, it's not me, I'm the already dead one, it's him
Looking at his last few frames of the present world
like the head of a cow blinking in a washtub
I watched him shed his soul like old skin
rising from the slumped lifeless body

"Want to come with me?" she asked, holding the
smoking pistol barrel down against the side of her leg.
"I had to waste him sooner or later and there's
nothing like the present tense when it comes to
getting even and the bastard had it coming.
We'll hike out to the highway and catch a ride
with the first truck that's going our way."
"No," I said, "don't worry about me, you go on
I'll stay here and watch his lurking soul vaporise at sunset.
When he wanders over the void, I'll be waiting."

I didn't have the heart to tell her she was coming on
to the already dead. She said, it was all right because
if I wasn't officially dead she'd have to kill me
sooner or later, like she did him in, for the thrill
I showed her that when I walked I left no footprints
in the soft fields of sand, so nobody could follow
When she pulled the trigger three times
I smiled while the slugs passed right through me.

DEAD EYES AT SUNDOWN

An aversion to the times
the faded act of age acting up
like the old man
who forgot to die
and lay about
the institution so long
they named a wing after him
never understanding why

He was always there
waiting for his appointment
never out of sight
worse than a visitor
who (for some unknown
reason) won't go home
death is no excuse
some wag suggested

no wilderness left
only the remoteness
of humanity

THE WIND THAT TOOK THE ROOF

One night the wind came
and took the roof away
the neighbours phoned
to say that grey shingles
were dealt around town
like decks of cards
in a game of fish lasting
less than five minutes
then the rain came in
and ruined the icing
on the poppy seed cake
driving the long haired cat
down into the basement
where it hid behind
the washing machine
finishing its spin cycle

In the morning the lawn's
greener than yesterday
that's for sure with more
dandelions blooming
than ever before
naked sky lurks overtly
above wide open rafters
long legged preening
birds peer straight in
from dizzy tree tops
for some unknown reason
at an undetermined time
the sun stopped ticking
and the landscape turned
itself out like an unmade
bed with itchy blankets

IMMACULATE FOOTWEAR

Marching all that way into heaven
wearing the wrong pair of loafers
A pair of spike high heels in front of St Peter
might be a bit a of shocker for the old boy's
heart when he sees the rest of your gear
If there ever was a time for clean underwear
neatly clipped toe nails and filed calluses
The old duffers who are ready for the walk
down the endless miles of red carpet
undoubtedly have old peoples' feet
creaking and groaning like ancient trees
about to come down in the forest

A man I know wearing pyjamas
and lightweight bedroom slippers
while waiting years for an appointment
for his ultimate accountability
looked silly in the grocery store
or in the gas station filling his tank
Guess he figured God would let
him hang around in the house
I've got it from a reliable source there's
a lot of walking in the after world

Sensible shoes might be the ticket
to show you're ready for the highway
or the big stairs to the penthouse floor
By the way nobody has to learn to kick
field goals to get into paradise
football boots are not practical
since God has decided to make
field goals automatically good
no matter from how far out.
Rubber thongs are a good idea
because of the slippery tile floors

BEDBUGS IN LOVE

Imagine living
in the erotic zone
between the sheets
in a bed in a classy
downtown hotel
patrons feed
bedbugs in love
just as love feeds
itself frenzied flesh
nerve ends dine
on sweaty candy

Bedbugs hump
like hump backed
overfed creatures
everywhere
proletarian
pleasures
fuelled by hot
bloody feasts
in silk sheets
even the lowly
bedbug does
it in real style

BOTTOMLESS

In a time of profound sadness
humour spills a glass of beer
into an innocent person's lap
a sudden momentary respite
from contemplating disaster
despite tear stained faces
laughter crashes the party
life needs a sweeter ingredient
than abject sorrow to appreciate
the depth of the emotional lake
laughter puts ripples on the pond

What if all the stars in the night sky
were lice in a black fur legacy
in an ultra violet universe
and we earthy creatures
merely robotic amoebas
in our smarmy little imaginations
as we multiply on a living host
When the beast comes awake
stomping off into the next oblivion

Leaving footprints in the mind
for psychic palaeontologists
digging under extinct oceans
in a world so dead and gone
that locating a single flounder
on the bottom of a shallow seabed's
about as profound an idea
as finding an unknown planet
in the bottom of a highball glass

I 'm crazy with scenarios working
over the boundaries of incendiary
thought in a world without fire
nothing here ever blows up
always the sound of wind passing
through compliant bending trees
the structure does not break easily
when it does it grows again
roots reach deep into bottomless

DYLAN THOMAS'S PARROT

The seventy year
old parrot speaks
the same Welsh
dialect as its master
who is more friend
than owner although
he has the power
to sell the naughty bird
that won't stop singing
like Tom Jones

When the pet shop
buyer insists
the bird must sound
like Mick Jagger
or the deal's off
the damn bird
won't stop singing
the "Green Green
Grass Of Home"

There is irony
in that voice
and inflections
from a hundred
generations
of tin miners

When the owner
takes the bird
home it begins
reciting Richard
Burton's lines
from "Who's Afraid
of Virginia Wolf"

AN ARGUMENT LIKE A BROKEN BONE

What is black and blue
and hides like a wounded
snake in the grass?

While the humble brain
tries vainly to sort the files
the ego is out taking
another ten rounds of self-
inflicted punishment

It pastes a frozen smile
on every slippery conversation
while the gears and wires
grumble, stretch and tremble
planets whirl overhead
in an insect galaxy Einstein
found about as complicated
as his grandmother's cuckoo clock

Fruit flies faithful as sugar
commit suicide by getting drunk
and crawling into half
empty wine bottles

Can you blame them?
what else is there to do
when you're a fat little
flying machine hatched
on the back of a sexy pineapple
that came by boat from Hawaii
and landed on the ice highway

Nothing to do but give it up
in an alcoholic haze

AT BOTH ENDS

Saw you coming and going
waited for you to say hello
nursing my drink for the road
watched the ice melt away
until there was nothing left
but to follow the way home

I came along the treed street
no magic left in empty eyes
only a big dose of cold truth
meaning cannot be translated
from our ancient conversations
the words are merely sounds

INTERIOR WILDERNESS

Time grows heavy in the flesh
weak, faltering along the limbs
sad, worn-out, punished feet
tireder than children ever get
slower than molasses on a cold day
no matter how far the tide goes out
the clam shell's never far from the clam

Sight, sound and taste decline
into a has-been trio of dullards
reassembled to advise an ancient brain
more things than ever are duller
than a broken pencil jabbed into an eye
even then, thoughts are far entwined
in grave recollections and some regret

Everybody remembered fondly, gone
down a back road about half a century
ago in a decade when time nearly stood
still in the shadows on summer evenings
compared to the way it weighs now
dropping a stone into blue water
future's a deep breath in darkness

Not so deep as to cause trauma
on a frail structure turning over
under the heavy blanket of sleep
before the eternal lights come on
blinding the bewildered mind
a warning like a factory whistle
tells the soul it's nearly time to go

Allan Safarik was born in Vancouver and raised in a commercial fishing family. He grew up in North Burnaby and spent much of his early life on Vancouver wharves when he wasn't playing soccer. Safarik is a prolific author in several genres. In 1986 he edited the award winning anthology Vancouver Poetry (Polestar Press). Safarik won the 2003 John V. Hicks manuscript Award for Literary Non-fiction and the Saskatchewan Book Award for Poetry in 2005 for When Light Falls from the Sun. Safarik currently teaches writing at St Peter's College in Muenster, Saskatchewan.